There is Power in Obedience

Vanessa Moore

Copyright © 2009 by Vanessa Moore

There is Power in Obedience
by Vanessa Moore

Printed in the United States of America

ISBN 978-1-60791-346-7

All rights reserved solely by the author. The author guarantees all contents are original and do not infringe upon the legal rights of any other person or work. No part of this book may be reproduced in any form without the permission of the author. The views expressed in this book are not necessarily those of the publisher.

Unless otherwise indicated, Bible quotations are taken from The King James Version.

www.xulonpress.com

Acknowledgements

First and foremost, I give thanks to God for my life and the opportunity to share the experiences of this journey. Thank you for your Son, Jesus, your Word, your spirit and unmerited favor. For these I am eternally grateful. I am also grateful to and for the people you have placed in my life, past and present, whom have inspired me and helped me along the way. To my loving husband, Keith: Without your love and support I could not have done this. I thank God for giving me a strong man of God with whom to share this journey. Our children, Ian and Austin, are two very unique people who will grow into mighty men of God one day. Your lives remind me that God is able and faithful. I want you to know that God is faithful to HIS word. Let Him lead and you follow Him.

To my siblings — Leola Hayes, Lela McCulley, Irene Paige, Caroline Thomas, and Christopher Thomas — may God bless each of you and your families. Much love to all my nieces and nephews.

To Tyra Wright: Girl, people would not be able to read this book if it wasn't for you! Thank you for your time and patience.

Regarding my church family, what can I say? You are REAL SAINTS! Faith Covenant Fellowship, thank you for all your support, prayers and LOVE. My Pastors Jay and E'dee Gregory are the best spiritual parents a child of God could want. Thank you for equipping me for my purpose! May God continue to bless you. For my two special friends who hung with us ALL the way — Frank & Margaret McGinnis – I love you. To BB, Lori, Chris and everybody else who helped along the way, may God Bless You ALL.

Much love and thanks!
Vanessa

Dedications

Gone but not forgotten are Louise Harmon, a great and special grandmother that God placed in my life and my parents, Julius and Mahalia Thomas. Thank you for teaching me how to live for Christ.

Table Of Contents

Introduction xi

Chapter One: Teach Me 13

Chapter Two: Speak Up 23

Chapter Three: Got Faith 33

Chapter Four: Wait Here 43

Chapter Five: As They Went 57

Introduction

As Christians, our testimony is usually given after we have come through a crisis. We testify most often in a church setting where believers are shouting, crying and giving praises to God Almighty for the manifestation of a blessing. It's exciting, but what about the difficult days? What about the rough nights? What keeps us going? What did the person who is testifying really do to overcome? What weapons are in their arsenal? What weapons did they use? When I was going through those were some of the questions that ran across my mind when I heard others' testimonies. God taught me in the seasons of my life that obedience unleashes the power that moves his hand.

As you read the pages of this book I pray that you will grow in faith and obedience as God takes you form glory to glory. Know God is faithful to his word.

Be Blessed!

Chapter One

TEACH ME

Show me thy ways, O Lord ; teach me thy paths

Psalms 25:4

TEACH ME

In our first home our lawn was ruined by grub worms. Now I don't know if you are familiar with these little creatures, but they eat the roots of your lawn, killing the yard underground while the lawn still appears to be in good shape on the surface. (That is the condition in which most Christians allow the devil to leave them.) Our lawn was in bad shape. When you walked on the grass, it would shift under your feet. You could kick the grass across the street, leaving bare dirt. We needed a new lawn and we had to do something fast and we were working with a budget. So we prayed about it. We quickly got an answer from the Holy Spirit. He said: "I want to teach you how to use the power of agreement. I want you and Keith to look out over the yard and speak out what you want." So we did.

We asked for sod, a sprinkler system, solar lights and a retaining wall. The next day there came a circular paper from the local garden center. The brick I needed was on sale. The price: $1.69 a brick! I went to the garden center to buy the brick. The sales people kept asking me: "Where did you get this paper?" I told them that it was delivered in the mail. Why were they asking? The brick in the advertisement was not the brick that was on sale. The brick I was inquiring about was $3.69 a brick. I was also a type of commercial brick. Eventually they sent me to a manager. The manager said the paper was a misprint but that he would honor it. "How many do you want?"

If I had not listened to what the spirit was trying to teach me, I would have missed out on my blessing. The same thing happened with the sod. I went to the nursery where my neighbor got his sod and paid $200 less then he did for the same size yard. The same thing happened with the sod and sprinkler system. I started getting estimates for the work, then learned one of our church members had a friend who did that kind of work. He gave us a great deal because of our mutual friend. We got everything that we asked for the yard.

Favor will always follow obedience! When you start to listen to the Holy Spirit, he will teach you what to do. It is his job. Teaching requires at least two individuals: the teacher and the student. The Holy Spirit is our teacher. His job is to lead us and guide us into all truth. We become students when we develop a willingness to learn and the discipline to listen. In fact, our progress depends on listening to instructions and a willingness to apply what we have heard.

I remember when, as a young student, I was trying to learn the multiplication table. The teacher kept saying that it was addition done in a faster way.

There is Power in Obedience

She then proceeded to break down the problem, step by step. That is what the Holy Spirit does. He breaks down the problem, step by step. Then he takes us through it. He tells us what to do, how to do it, and when to do it. If we are willing to follow his orders, we will see more progress in our Christian growth.

At this point in my life I did not know much to do, but pray. Often that wasn't enough. I wasn't sure of the words to say. Eventually, I learned to pray the Word of God. I started searching the Bible for everything that I was going through. Then I quoted the Word over my situation.

The devil does not have any power over you. He has only the power that you allow him. I remember the Holy Spirit saying that he would teach me the power of agreement. My husband and I were in agreement in some ways, but we had to be in agreement with the Word of God, according to the scriptures.

God wants to be a father to us. We are his children; he loves us and wants to take care of us. As his children, we must learn what the Father expects from us. As earthly parents, we want love, obedience, loyalty and quality time together. So does God. I believe we Christians sometimes let our natural senses convince us that we need a physical teacher. Just think how many times the Spirit tried to tell you not to do something, but you overruled that thought and did it anyway. Have you ever started working on a project and something said there is a better and more efficient way to do the very same thing? That's the Holy Spirit trying to "teach" you. Reading God's Word also helps teach you. The more you read and mediate on the Word, the better chance you have in becoming victorious.

In 1 John 2:27, the scriptures state: "But the anointing which you have received from Him abides in you, and you do not need that anyone teach you; but as the same anointing teaches you concerning all things, and is true, and is not a lie and just as it has taught you, you will abide in Him."

So see, you are not alone. God did not leave anything out concerning our growth process. We just don't like to be told what to do. As I began to look around at my circumstances I knew that God wanted more for me. I just did not know where to start. Then one day as I was reading my Bible I came across this passage of scripture in Matthew 7:8: "For everyone who asks receives, and he who seeks finds, and to him knocks it will be opened." This was the beginning of a journey that taught us so much about God and our selves.

"Teach Me" Strategies

If you want to be taught His way of doing things, you will have to ask yourself to serious, and maybe even difficult, questions. What are we learning on a daily basis? If I am asking, why haven't I received? If I am seeking, why have I not found anything? Why does every door seem to be closed to me? Sound familiar? Take a few moments and write down at least three questions that you have asked God concerning your circumstances.

1.

2.

3.

Now, get your Bible and see if you can find what the Word says about your circumstance(s). Don't get frustrated while looking; remember this is your life!

If your Bible gives you cross reference scriptures, read them too. During this process you will learn to search for your solution in the Word of God. Then the Holy Spirit can deposit more easily this information into your spirit. The information may become very valuable in the future because there may come a time in your life when the reference scriptures may come in handy. At those times the Holy Spirit will bring them to your remembrance Now let's try another exercise.

Take the scriptures that you have found and write them down five times. Read them to yourself at least twice a day for two or three weeks. Now you are in the process of memorizing scriptures and renewing your mind at the same time. Christianity is a process; developing your Christian walk will require time, effort and patience.

Now that you have some answers according to the Word of God about your circumstances, what are you going to do about it? Will you allow the Holy Spirit to do help you to achieve what God promised you or will you continue to go your own way? The choice is always yours.

Remember, you have to follow the guidelines of the Holy Spirit. You are not leading anymore. You want to see results, right? Then invest time in getting to know God and yourself. Be honest about the things you don't know. Ask questions. Develop the habit of writing things down. Get organized. You will be surprised at the amount of time you waste not being organized. Time management is so important. A lot of our blessings are time sensitive. There are windows of opportunities for a specific time or season. The Holy Spirit allows us to move supernaturally.

Consider Psalms 25:4. You must ask the Lord to show you and teach you His ways. Don't worry about how long you have been doing things until this point. Focus on the new and fresh. Just like in the story at the beginning of the chapter where my husband and I were guided, step by step by the Holy Spirit, you too can be guided, step by step, in the things of God. That incident with the lawn was the first time as a couple that we were combining our faith. I had been a Christian for a number of years before my husband. I had been praying for him to become a Christian for 13 years! During that time the Holy Spirit taught me how to witness to my husband and win him over for Christ. The most important part of my witness was my lifestyle. He saw the results on the outside of the work the Spirit was doing on the inside of me.

Learning can be a very fun experience when you decide to be a willing participant. To the contrary, you could be one of those people who repeat the same lesson over and over getting nowhere. Make up in your mind today that you want the Holy Spirit to teach you everything you need to enjoy life according to God's plan and purpose for you. It will change for life for the better. You have nothing to lose and everything to gain.

Chapter Two

SAY WHAT

You shall declare a thing, And it will be established for you

Job 22:28a

SAY WHAT

The reason most Christians live such defeated lives is that they do not know the right words to say in order to be victorious. That is why it is important to become skilled in the Word of God. We have power. Power, however, that has no directions or is used improperly is useless. Speaking the word of God is powerful and the more you practice using it correctly the more skillful you become. We are to declare things for we are priest. Jesus has given us power over the enemy. Therefore, we have the right and the authority to use it. The Lord deals with our mouths because out of mouths comes either blessings or curses. Proverbs 18:21 will confirm that statement.

I became convinced that I had to learn to speak up. I began to read about the promises of God for his children and I started to wonder why have not experienced some of these promises. I was taught that God does not and can not lie. I felt like Gideon. "Where are the promises," I said to myself.

My husband and I decided to start confessing the promises of God out loud and to be in agreement and focus on our pursuit. Matthew 16:19 states: "And I will give you the keys of the kingdom of heaven. And whatever you bind on earth will be bound in heaven, and whatever you loose on earth will be loosed in heaven." Isn't it funny how we can go to sports arenas and be as loud as we can cheering for our team to win, but we don't come to church and cheer for our team to win? You do know we win in the end, middle and beginning? We are to be a living testimony showing forth the glory of God. I would not share the goodness of God unless I was around other Christians because I thought they would understand and glorify the Lord with me. I did not know that my testimony could be used as a tool for winning souls to Christ. God will give you boldness if you ask for it.

I started teaching my children the importance of confessions and confessing. As we confessed, we admitted having done something wrong, some kind of error. We then spoke our confessions openly without hindrance. Our mouth can be our biggest downfall. Under the control of the Holy Spirit, it can be our most powerful weapon. It's time for us as believers to speak up and out loud for the kingdom, to have the power and authority to be the sons and daughters the world is waiting for. Come on; let's make some noise!

I am a firm believer that what you say will affect your life. Speaking the Word of God is powerful. The more you practice using the Word correctly, the more

There is Power in Obedience

skillful you become in it. According to Proverbs 18, 21, "Death and life are in the power of the tongue, and those who love it will eat its fruit."

Relive your past victories and testimonies. It will give you confidence and increase your faith to believe that God is able to do whatever you need him to do in your life. This is what is meant in Revelation 12:11: "And they overcame him by the blood of the lamb, and the words of their testimony." Any time you have a chance to share your testimony, share it. It's a double blessing. You receive a blessing for sharing and the hearer gets an opportunity to be encouraged by listening. Consider your trials and tribulations an opportunity to effectively speak the Word of God to change your circumstances. Instead of praying about your problems as if God doesn't have a clue, pray the promises of God. Refer to those things that do not exist as though the do exist. Are your skeptical? Consult Romans 4:17b.

Watch what you say! Let your words be positive and edifying. Keep all idle and negative words out of your vocabulary. Hang around positive people, no dream killers. Negative people can give you 100 reasons why you shouldn't want the things you desire.

Guard your heart. Remember out of it flows the issues of life. Don't forget to praise God for the promises. Many times we make the mistake of praising God after we receive our blessings. No, we have to have faith to give thanksgiving before we see it.

Learn to incorporate the names of God in your prayers. There is power in the names of God. For example: Jehovah Jireh, which means He is the Lord our Provider; Jehovah Rapha, the Lord that heals us, and Jehovah Rohi, the Lord who is my Shepherd. Practice praying these names and then find other names to add into your prayers.

Get a prayer partner. Where two or three gather together in agreement in His name, He is in the midst, according to Matthew 18:19-20. There is power in partnership. I remember my prayer partner and I use to go by the river in the summertime and pray out loud. We were radical and serious about our prayer time, but we got results! Don't forget what you are fighting for and stay focused. Remember the devil does not fight fair, and he's on his job 24/7. He has studied you for years. He knows you so you must step up your game. You are not alone. Heaven is cheering you on and Jesus is making intercession for you. You can do it. Now let's get started. Your mouth will have to be trained to speak the word of GOD over all your circumstances.

A typical prayer that goes something like this: "Lord you know I need help down here. I've got these bills to pay. Money is low. Please bless me in my finances. Bless me with a job or a better one. Oh Lord, I need you NOW! Help me with my children. Help me to meet all our needs. I pray AMEN."

That sounds okay. But let's put some power to that same prayer by using the Word of GOD:

> Spirit of the living God I worship you in spirit and in truth. No weapon formed against me shall prosper and every tongue that rises up

against me shall be condemned, so declares the Word of the God. I thank you that you have made known your thought towards me, thoughts of good things and blessings for me and not of evil. I thank You Father that I am blessed with a sound mind, with the peace that passes all understanding. I thank you for being the God who helps me. I take authority over Satan in the name of Jesus. I come against every evil and hindering spirit of the enemy. I bind them from my life and the lives of my family, and I render them powerless. Helpless, and ineffective to hinder, delay or stop God's plan and purpose in my life in any way, by the authority of the name of Jesus Christ. I pull down every stronghold of the enemy. I cast down every wicked imagination that Satan would attempt to use in the name of Jesus. Now Father I thank you for Your Word does not return unto you void, but it accomplishes the things you send it to perform. Father, I have prayed your word. I thank you for performing Your Word in my life and in the lives of my family. In the name of our Lord and Savior Jesus Christ I pray. Amen.

See how the scriptures come alive. You're no longer focused on the problems, but you pray the promises. Get in your Bible, saints! Write your own confessions and prayers based on the Word of God.

"The grass wither, the flower fadeth: but the word of God shall stand forever," states Isaiah 40:8. Now that's power. Let me share with you this little story that I recently went through. My husband and I dropped off our taxes to be done for 2007. Now usually it only takes about a week for them to be completed. After about three weeks I called our tax person to see if our tax returns were done. We were told that we owed the government about $10,000. I said, "When were you going to tell us?" Now I haven't worked in two or three years, only part-time off and on. I didn't make that much money.

We began to speak out the promises of God over our situation. I asked the Lord to expose the enemy and reveal to me the truth. Over the next few weeks we worked with the tax preparer almost daily. We discovered that we did not owe the Federal government anything but we did owe the State of Michigan. We prayed and we paid.

"Say What" Strategies

What do you do when trouble comes? What is your first response? Make sure that you keep your words positive and full of faith. Check the words coming out of your mouth. No doubt, don't doubt! Guard your heart. Even as I am writing to you now, the Federal government has audited our 2006 income taxes. They claim that they over paid us but to God be the glory. We will not fear! I'll let you know in the next book the outcome of that situation. Until then, speak up!

A confession is stating the Word of God over the circumstances in your life to line up according to the promises of God. The goal is to come into agreement with God's Word. According to 1Timothy 6:12, "Fight the good fight of faith, lay hold on eternal life, to which you were also called and have confessed the good confession in the presence of many witnesses.

Compose your own confession using the Word of God. In your personal confession, declare those things that you want to see. Write down your confession so that you can repeat it daily. Remember to be bold, positive and focused as you develop your confession.

Chapter Three

GOT FAITH

But without faith it is impossible to please Him, for he who comes to God must believe that He is a rewarder of those who diligently seek Him.

Hebrews 11:6

GOT FAITH

This journey started off with a leap of faith that challenged me in every area of my Christian walk. I know we all say we trust God with our very life, but do we really? What if you were put in a position for a period of time where you had to depend on God for everything? That's what happened to me and my family.

One day in the fall of 2003, I was in the basement of my home doing the laundry when the Holy Spirit said to me: "Do you trust me?"

"Yes, Lord, I trust you."

"No, do you really trust me?" asked the Spirit.

"Yes, Lord, I really, do."

Then the Spirit said, "I'm going to have to put you in a position where you have to really trust me."

I told my husband about the visitation that I had received from the Holy Spirit. We prayed for strength for whatever the Lord was going to do to us. Then about two weeks later I woke up one morning by a voice that told me to start packing my bedroom first, only leave out three sets of bed linen. So I began to pack as I was told to do. I didn't ask any questions, I just did it. I knew in my spirit that God was moving. I didn't want to abort any promises nor cause any delays. I just kept praying for wisdom, knowledge and understanding in the things of God. But all I got was peace.

Sometimes God will not let you know what is going on at the start of things, but He will give you a peace about them. It will make sense in due season. As I began to pack up the things in the house, the instructions on what to do became more frequent and precise. Soon I just got up in the mornings and continued where I left off. After about a month of packing, I received a telephone call. My aunt was sick and in the hospital. Now, my aunt was in her 90s, living by herself in a senior citizen apartment building. So I went to the hospital to visit her. She was incoherent. I was told that they were going to send her to a rehab center or a nursing home because she could not go back to her apartment. There had been an incident where she gave her keys to a stranger. Another time, she was lost in the building and could not remember how to get to her apartment.

My aunt and I have always had a great relationship. I spent lots of time with her as a child and as an adult. Before I was married, I told my husband I was a package deal. I explained that I had this aunt who has no children and if anything ever happened to her I must take care of her. He agreed.

The hospital started giving her experimental treatments because she had no advocate or legal guardian. I had to go to court to declare her incompetent and become her legal guardian. I took her home to live with me. Now I was working the midnight shift in a hospital where I had been employed for over 20 years. As soon as I gave them my guardianship papers over my aunt, my boss started treating me differently. The director of the department asked me why I would do something like that. She explained that they have places for people in her condition. I told them it was my decision and I wanted to take care of my aunt if I was able to do so.

Now you know sometimes your assignment from God comes in a way and time when you least expect it. I had asked God years ago that if my aunt ever got to the point where she could not care or herself to allow me to care for her. And that is what He did. What I didn't know was how good God would be during this time.

At work my boss was constantly on my back. My house was this small, three bedroom bungalow with one bathroom. My boys had to move into a room together. (That wasn't so bad because they had bunk beds.) But my aunt needed a hospital bed and she did not have health insurance. I had to apply for assistance from a state agency. We received $10 each month in food assistance benefits, nothing else. My aunt had a prescription that cost $147 each month. But, God, thank you! God sent word through the Holy Spirit to tell me that he would show me how to take care of my aunt without asking for a dime. And I did it, too. I was able to come up with a budget with the help of the Holy Spirit to take care of all her needs. My niece had an old hospital bed in her garage that she gave me. I was able to fit it into our van. Later, I found a physician that made house calls to the elderly. He wrote a prescription for an air hospital bed for my aunt. Her Medicare covered half the cost and the company wrote off the other half as a hardship based on my aunt's income. Favor! I made sure that I sent my aunt's tithes to her church every month. She had not been a tither, but I am so she was too when she lived with me.

One Tuesday evening during praise and worship at our church, the Spirit said, "You're needed at home." He said that I was not going back to work.

"Resign."

"What?"

I took a few days off work because I was stressed from the pressure of caring for my aunt and pressure from the job also. But this was a big step. This isn't just about me; it involves my family too. I started thinking about my bills, buying food, caring for my aunt and everything else. Then I remembered the fall of 2003. I asked God to give me signs if this is really him speaking to me. I went on a three-day fast to get my answer from God and to get strength for what I had to do. I went to my pastor and told him what the Lord was telling me to do. My pastor asked how much money I made last year. I told him and he said that's a seed. My spirit leaped because I understood the principal of sowing and reaping. I got excited and bold. I decided to step out on faith and resign. Yes, you guessed it. The adversary came right away. Isn't that just like him always trying to come against what

God is trying to do for you? He comes with fear, doubt and unbelief as his choice weapons.

I went to work and turned in m resignation. As I got on the elevator, I could hear the devil say "you fool, turn around." But I kept going. The doors of the elevator opened again. The enemy said: "Run, stupid. Nobody saw you just turn around and leave." At this point, I knew that it wasn't about me anymore; it was all about God and His plan and purpose for my life. What He was going to do for me didn't involve my help, but he did need my cooperation. My faith was really tried during this time. I won't tell you that I wasn't scared because I was. My faith in God got me through it.

I remembered that my mother taught me a scripture when I was about 16 years old. Proverbs 3: 5-6 had become one of my favorites and has gotten me through plenty. "Trust in the Lord with all your heart, and lean no on your own understanding; in all your ways acknowledge Him, and he shall direct your path."

As I acknowledge God in the situation he began to direct me regarding what I should do. The more I obeyed, the more he proved Himself to me, the more confident I became in the things of God I could believe the things the Holy Spirit spoke to me because my faith was increasing. I had started a relationship with God. God wants to have a living, personal relationship with you. He desires for us to tell him the things that bother us as well as the things that make us happy, not because He does not know, but because it creates intimacy with Him.

Intimacy reveals secrets. God can share with you and your sharing with Him brings deliverance into your life. That is a whole other chapter in a future book. The key thing is communication, the freedom to express your self to someone and to have that someone understand you. I don't know about you but I find that refreshing. It takes faith to operate in intimacy with God. You have to believe that what you are telling God will make a difference in your life and that God is interested in hearing what you have to say.

"Got Faith" Strategies

Ask yourself the following questions. Have I operated in faith that has bought any real change in my life? In what area have I not been willing to give God my full cooperation? Do I really have the faith to trust God?

If your answers to these questions trouble you, here are a few suggestions. Start with a fast. Fasting and prayer are always attached to each other. Fasting is a voluntary abstinence from food. It is a strategy of the gospel of Jesus Christ for developing spiritual strength. It has always existed among true believers. It is part of disciplining the body and reminding the body that it is not in charge.

Fasting is a good way to put your flesh under submission to prepare your spirit to receive from God. God's Word will always challenge you to bring out the best that He has put inside of you. We are being challenged every day of our lives to make a choice whether to trust God in all that we do, personally, physically and financially. What do you have to lose by placing everything in God's hands? He is more capable of caring for us than we are caring for ourselves.

Matthew 6:16 states "And whenever you are fasting, do not look gloomy and sour and dreary like hypocrites, for they put on a dismal countenance, that their fasting may be apparent to and seen by men. Truly I say to you, they have their reward in full already."

Prayer is communication with God. It is the words that are spoken to verbalize thoughts, intents, concerns, and desires. It does not mean that we do all the talking. God has to have His say too.

Philippians 4:6 says "Be anxious for nothing, but in everything by prayer and supplication, with thanksgiving, let your request be made known to God."

Fast and pray!

Deborah Walker
37674 Copperstone Dr.
Sterling Hts., MI 48312-4810

Chapter Four

WAIT HERE

*Wait on the Lord; Be of good courage,
And He shall strengthen your heart;
Wait I say on the Lord.*

Psalm 27:14

WAIT HERE

Sometimes when you are waiting on God, He will lead you to do things that seem foolish or totally opposite from the world's way of doing things. In 2005 my husband's grandmother had gone home to be with the Lord. She left her home to my husband. It was a two-bedroom frame ranch style house with a basement. My husband was planning to sell it to investors because he did not want to be bothered with renting the property. He also was not ready to clean out the house. One day the Spirit told me that Keith wasn't ready for that; it was my job.

So for about a month my children and I cleaned out the house. We got help from relatives and from our church family too. After we got the house cleaned, I had an idea to use it as a resale shop. Every day I would go over to the house, open it up and put out my sign. No customers! One day I was in the basement of the house looking around and the Holy Spirit said, "I didn't have you clean this house to make a store out of it. I want you all to move over here and sell your house."

"Oh, Lord, I can't tell my husband that," was my response. "Lord, you are going to have to tell my husband."

God honored my request. A couple days later my husband came home from work and, while I was cooking, he started talking about what we should do with grandma's house. I got silent. He said he wanted to sell it. I was still silent. Then he had this strange look on his face. I asked him, "What is it?" He said, "I just got a thought dropped into my spirit. It's crazy."

"Just say it," I told him.

"We could move into the house and sell our house."

"That's exactly what we are going to do because that's what the Spirit told me three days ago," I said.

You see, God will respect and honor your request when you are in right standing with him. I didn't know how to tell my husband. I did not know if he would be ready to receive that word. But the Holy Spirit knew that Keith was ready to receive it. We moved in the house by the end of July that same year.

The scripture at 1 Corinthians 2:14 says, "But the natural man does not receive the things of the Spirit of God, for they are foolishness to him; nor can he know them, because they are spiritually discerned." I quoted that scripture because when we packed up and moved the Spirit spoke again: "Don't take anything from Egypt with you." So we gave everything away. Our family and friends could not believe that we were moving into a smaller house in a not so great neighborhood, but we did.

It took the longest time for us to move. We had lived in our house for 17 years. We had accumulated a lot of stuff. Every day for at least a month, we were moving things. The children got tired of boxing up belongings and so did we. Yet, it had to be done. There was no one else to do it but us. Finally, the day came when we were completely done. Still, we had to check weekly on the house. Now we had to wait for our next set of instructions from the Lord.

Year One

I was determined to make our wait smooth. I was concerned about two teenage boys, a cat, and two small bedrooms. Did I mention it was small, smaller than where we moved from and we had outgrown that house? So my husband and I decided to give each child his own room. My husband and I slept in the living room on a sofa bed. During that time, we were preparing out house for sale. We did most of the work ourselves. We did all the painting, laid a new floor, installed light fixtures and did the land scraping. We would work on the house whenever we got time. God blessed us to have friends to help us get things together.

But as soon as we got busy doing what God had instructed us to do, the devil got busy too. He started messing with the family, the children first. Please remember to guard your family with prayers that are aimed at the problem you are facing. You can do this by looking in your Bible and finding scriptures that will aid you in the fight. Turn those scriptures into prayers. Put the Word of God, not your words, on the situation.

See, that is what the Word of God in Isaiah 55:11 tells us: "So shall My word be that goes forth from My mouth; It shall not return to Me void, But it shall accomplish what I please, And it shall prosper in the thing for which I sent it." It is what God says about the situation that counts. You have to be in agreement with His Word. This was a lesson that I had learned through our season. Now, I am passing it on to you. When God starts you in the direction of your destiny, you will run into some obstacles along the way. Later, I found out that those very obstacles would help me stay focused on the bigger picture.

We started confessing the Word daily out loud. The reason I said to quote them out loud is to make a statement, to serve notice on the devil by putting it in the atmosphere. Your words have power. USE IT! What you say about your circumstance will determine your outcome. "Death and life are in the power of the tongue, And those who live it will eat its fruit," instructs Proverbs 18:21.

We put our house up for sale during a difficult time to sell homes, but God said it and we believed Him. During this time, we did not have any buyer interested in our house. We took the house off the market. We started praying, asking God if we had missed something. If so, show us. He told us to go back to the house and finish the work on it. We put a new roof on the house. We also hired an electrician to install new lights and light switches for the upstairs. The Holy Spirit told us, "don't sow anything that

There is Power in Obedience

we weren't willing to reap. We sold our home that fall. We gave the new owners everything the Lord told us to leave for them. We left the stove, refrigerator, freezer, washer and dryer and much more. After we did that, God blessed us to get out of debt completely.

But on the flip side, the enemy started acting out in our oldest child. He got kicked out of school for his behavior. Now, I had to find him a school to go to really fast. I put my children in the neighborhood school. That was very challenging physically and spiritually. I cried daily. One time right in the mist of my tears, the Lord spoke. "Speak my Word over them." He told me that my children had to see where they had been in order to appreciate where I am going to take them. I started putting anoint oil in the laundry when I washed their school uniforms. I prayed confessions over them at night.

I had taken a job 30 miles away from our home to help out a friend. It was a part-time position and the pay was fine. One day while I was at work, I received a telephone call from the Detroit police. The officer said that there had been an altercation involving some boys and my son. My son was injured during the encounter as these boys tried to rob him. One boy had a knife and cut my son under his eye. Now, this could not have happened if my son had not sneaked out of the house, breaking our rules in the process. I told my son that is how it is. When you don't do as you are told, you are not under the covering of God. You are unprotected and leave yourself open for the devil to come in and wreak havoc on you. My children made it through the rest of the school year without any problems. That summer our mission was to find a home so that in the fall the children would be in a new school. Not so despite the fact that every Saturday my husband and I went looking.

Waiting on the Lord will require some patience. "But let patience have its perfect work, that you may be perfect and complete, lacking nothing," states James 1:4. I had to look for a new school for my children. Eventually, I enrolled my sons in two different schools and that took a toll on me. I resigned from the part-time job I had because my season was up. My friend that I was helping was very supportive. She had come to me and told me that the Spirit told her it was time for me to go because I had to get ready to move. Her words were another confirmation for us.

Now, my oldest son's school was 30 miles away from our home and the youngest son's school was in the opposite direction, about 20 miles away. God gave us favor that traffic was always smooth when picking up the children, even in the winter. I knew both principals at their schools so I did not worry about them when they were at school. We made it through the whole year.

We began to set the atmosphere in our home. We would allow praise music to play continually while away from the house. We played specific songs that had an anointing to saturate the house.

Year Two

"It has been two years, Lord, and we are still here!" That was our response at this point. The whole family was weary. In addition, the furnace stopped working. It was January! We still had three months of winter. A heating and cooling company said we needed a new furnace or we could put "a band aid" on the old one just to make it through the winter. This band aid would cause us $300. I told my husband about the band aid option along with the repairman's estimate for a new furnace. My husband said that he would look it over later. He wanted to pray about it first. The Lord gave us an answer and it was not what we expected. We were instructed not to get it fixed nor to buy a new one, but to trust God.

We decided that if we have come this far with God, we were going to go all the way to the end. After all, we have nothing to lose and everything to gain. The house would get very cold sometimes. Sleeping on a sofa bed by the window was very uncomfortable. My husband and I decided to buy space heaters for the children. One day I was in the basement washing clothes and decided to speak to the furnace. I told it I wanted heat. Then I laid hands on the furnace and the heat came on. That started something. Every time we wanted heat, we would command the furnace to bring it forth.

Just like heat, food, the appreciation of it, is a lesson our sons had to learn. They were very wasteful. My husband told me that while he was shopping one day, he started putting fewer items in the cart. He knew it was the Spirit telling him: "Don't buy a lot of stuff. Cut down on the amount of food you bring into the house. Then there won't be any waste." That is what he did.

Next, we started quoting the promises of God for our needs. In our giving offerings, seed in other words, to the church, we gave our seed an assignment. Our pastor told us it was our season. Believing God, we conclude that it was our season.

Sometimes, God will take you out of your comfort zone to see if you are grateful for just the simple things in life or are you just the type of Christian that can only praise Him when you have all your creature comforts. We learned how to make due with the things we had. We also had to budget our resources better. In Luke 12:42, Jesus said "who then is that faithful and wise steward, whom his master will make ruler of his household, to give them their portion of food in due season."

While we were going through our season, we served faithfully in our church. We are servants in the house of God. We must never forget that, saints. If we lose sight of our purpose because of trials and tribulations, how can we hold on to the manifestations that are birthed during them? We started looking at houses every Saturday with our pastor. Then late one night we got a call from a close family member. She told us that the Holy Spirit told her to tell us to get ready to move. "It's a done deal. God is working some things out on our behalf. Just go!" The next morning, the Holy Spirit woke me and told me three things. One, everything with my husband and I is time sensitive. Two, it is important that we do exactly what He says. Three, go get your house!

We were very excited. We went to our spiritual father and pastor with the instructions we had received from the Holy Spirit. It is important to have a spiritual covering to be able to talk with to help you discern what you are going through in your season. You don't want to fall into error or hearsay. Your shepherd knows his flock. God has equipped pastors to serve as spiritual parents to us. I am so glad to have Pastors Jay and E'dee in our lives. Our pastors helped guide us in the direction God had planned for us through their knowledge and wisdom. Don't be afraid to ask your pastors for help. There will be times in your life when the words of your shepherds will launch you into your destiny like a catapult. In addition, you may find that vital instructions come from your pastors. Our next instructions did. That is the way God had it set up. Our pastor had started taking us every Saturday to see homes.

During the time we spent with Pastor Jay, God was building us up. We learned a lot of things in our season. We learned patience, the importance of having the right confessions, sowing and reaping, tithing, fasting and praying, commitment and contentment. Obedience, however, was the key thing we learned. I questioned God several times in the storms that we faced. He didn't always give me an answer but sometimes he did.

Don't be afraid to ask God questions. You may receive great revelation. When God speaks to you, you will know. There is a peace that takes over and all fear and doubt disappears. Have faith in God. Believe that He will move mightily on your behalf. Stand boldly on his Word. We all have storms and wilderness experiences. Know that you are not alone. Other believers are going through similar trials and tribulations. You are in the best position for a miracle. Stay focused. Birthing a destiny takes work. The labor pains are signs your "baby" is ready to be born. Just make sure that you do everything to endure a successful delivery.

Not being where God sends you could cause you to lose what he has for you. Once, I dropped the children off at their friend's home. "I'll pick you up right here later." After several hours, I gave them a call. I told them I was on my way.

"Meet me where I dropped you off in twenty minutes."

When I arrived, I found no children. I waited for ten minutes before returning home. Five minutes later the children called. "Are you coming to get us?" Once I found out they were okay and nothing had happened to them, I asked "Where are you?" They had decided to go over to another friend's house without permission. As a result, they missed their ride because the other friend's house was further from the place where they were supposed to meet me than they thought. Consequently, missing their appointed time caused them to miss their blessing, a ride home. Don't miss your appointed time by not being where you are supposed to be.

"Wait Here" Strategies

You may at times feel impatient or disappointed. At these times, pull out your confession and remember that season may require you to be still for periods of time. There is still something you can do. Wait (for additional instructions) rest, and pray!

Chapter Five

AS THEY WENT

Thus also faith by itself, if it does not have works, is dead.

James 2:17

AS THEY WENT

This last chapter will hopefully be the start of or encourage you to continue your Christian walk. I have compiled testimony after testimony to show you what happens when you put your faith into action. Let's start with the story of the ten lepers found Luke 17: 12-14.

> Then as He entered a certain village, there met Him ten men who were lepers, who stood afar off. And they lifted up their voices and said "Jesus, Master have mercy on us!"
> So when he saw them, He said, "Go show yourself to the priests." And so it was that as they went, they were cleaned.

Wow! Just starting to act on the orders given by Jesus cleansed them. To get the results you are seeking you will have to do something. It requires action on your part. My husband and I knew that what we expected from God was going to take action and obedience on our part. It all started in 2005 when

I was told by the Holy Spirit to come off my job. I was afraid as I explained in chapter three, but I had to quit the job to get the things I wanted from God. I know that we think that at times we are giving up so much for something that has not happened yet nor do we know when it will happen or will it happen. That is the very thing that adversary wants you to keep pondering over and over in your head so that fear and doubt can set up shop in your heart and mind. Remember, without faith it is impossible to please God. In the scripture the ten lepers separated from the village people, but they too had a need. They lifted up their voices so that they would be heard by the Master. When the devil has you off to the side, you better make some noise! Send out an SOS in the spirit. Jesus heard the lepers and responded to their cry. He did not heal them instantly but gave them a command that if activated by their faith and obedience would bring a solution to their situation. God invites us to activate our faith through our obedience to His word, by trusting Him and conforming to His plans and purpose. God desires for us to prosper and be in good health even as our soul prospers, according to 2 John 3.

My husband and I believed God for a house in a specific area because of the school system for our two children. Now the Lord has showed me over 10 years ago in a dream that I would be moving into a bigger home that was beautifully decorated. It had all the things I desired to be in my home. I got excited and started looking at houses. But how many of you know that God is a God of seasons. And it was not my season for house hunting. It was a time for preparation. It took ten years for the manifestation, but God made it worth the wait. Now you may say ten years? I can't wait that long, and you may not have to either, but what if you do? What will you do? Be patient. Be obedient. Believe me I know from experiences that you can't bring your season any faster then God's appointed time. After all, you want it to be a blessing from God.

We learned that as we went, God made provision for us to have what we needed and wanted. The blessings were overtaking us. The very acts of obedience opened such great opportunities for us that we were able to walk through so many things with little or no resistance. Our praise and worship before the Lord had taken a new turn. We learned to praise God before the manifestations, and be grateful for the things that we possess. That's a big one right there. Learn to be happy and grateful for what you see every day. As we went to live in the place I call our "Kadesh," I was preparing for the promise land at the same time. I just knew that God was going to bless us real soon because we had moved to this place like he commanded us to and as a reward for our obedience, He would move us into our dream house.

Not so fast. We did not know that this would be a journey that lasted two years. Now during these two years, even though I was obedient to God, I had to get my attitude right, my servitude right and I had to be balanced. We had lived in our home for 17 years. I remember praying for that house, but now the Lord was telling me that he was preparing a place for us and we had to wait for Him to say, "Go!" I became frustrated many days and I learned how to pray out my frustrations in the spirit realm. I went to God with my heavy heart and feelings exposed to Him. I expressed to Him my thoughts, fears, worries, doubts and dreams. As I began to be more open about the way I felt, the more He began to speak to me. God wants to have a close relationship with you so that He can reveal things to you. See, God knows you are going to need encouragement and He is waiting to give it to you.

My husband and I began to quote the Word of God. We started putting His Word into action. Every promise that was spoken by the Holy Spirit we declared it to be so in the name of Jesus. Every instruction and direction we did without hesitation. We kept fasting, praying and sowing. We became bold in our faith. The devil is a bully. He tries to bully his way into our thoughts and emotions. After the tears, worry and sleepless nights, guess what? You're still going to have to fight. So, you might as well get your sleep so you can go the distance with him. That's a decision you will have to make quickly if you want the promises of God. David said it best in Psalm 37:5. "I have been young, and now old; yet I have never seen the righteous forsaken, nor his descendants begging bread." All while I was off work those two years we were never behind in any of our bills. We never fell behind on any payments and we went on vacation to Florida. We paid cash for that trip a year in advance.

We sold our home to a beautiful couple at our church. And the Lord allowed us to be a blessing to them by leaving them all the major appliances. We also bought them a brand new dining room set. We let them move into the house before they got approved for their mortgage because that is what the Lord wanted us to do. Now, in return for the seed that we sowed, this is what God did for us. He said, "Go get your house!" Go survey the land. In January 2007 we were house hunting with our pastor, who was our real estate agent. We had been looking at homes every weekend. We went and looked at new construction homes. Remember, I am not working. These homes were out of our budget. Seven days after seeing the house we call home, my husband calls me to ask me if we had $5,000 to put done on the house.

I asked, "What house?"

He said, "the house Pastor Jay showed us."

Again, I said, "Which one?"

"The new one!"

My husband told me that the Holy Spirit spoke to him and told him to build. So we went out that night and put the money down on the lot to build God's house. The Holy Spirit told us not to say anything until the house was done. For seven months, we did exactly what we were told to do. First, we were approved for the loan for the house. Then we went on vacation. When we returned we checked on the progress of the home. The sales agent for the builder told us that since we had not closed on our home yet that they were going to try to save us some money by reducing the price. So here we are in the sales office sitting while he redid the paperwork. He told us he has never seen this done before in all the years he has worked for the company. He came in with the papers and told us that the builder is taking $18,500 off the price of the house!!!! Just as he finished, I heard the Holy Spirit say, "Didn't I tell you that I would take care of you?" My husband and I were speechless. We ran to the house and started praising God. We began to thank Him for His faithfulness and blessings, and for the beautiful home that he was entrusting to us. Now, you know that the devil was mad about that and tried to stop it too. Two weeks before we were to close on our home, the adversary tried to make a grand stand move. We received a phone call from our sales agent. He said that the mortgage company was trying to get in contact with us. Up until now our mortgage company was contacting us every few weeks with no problems. We called the mortgage company and were told that we needed to find other financing because they were pulling out after approving us. Unless we bought cash, we could not get the house. "The devil is a liar," was my response. God stepped right in, on time as always. Five days before we were to close, a private bank came forth and financed us 100%. God will move mightily on behalf of those who are willing and obedient. I told the Lord: "This is your battle. We have done every thing you told us to do."

We stood on His Word and declared His promises. When we moved into our new home, God blessed us to buy everything brand new and pay cash for it all! To God be the Glory! There is great power in being obedient. I was able to experience one of my favorite scriptures, Ephesians 3:20. "Now to Him who is able to do exceedingly abundantly above all that we ask or think, according to the power that works in us."

We have the power working in us. That power is faith. Just like the lepers were healed as they went, when you get your orders, your blessing will come as you follow the orders.

"As They Went" Strategies

Obedience is the act of obeying. It is to acknowledge authority, to submit, to do what is asked of you and to follow orders. Philemon 21 states: "Having confidence in your obedience, I write to you. Knowing that you will do even more than I say."

Be blessed and obedient until next time.

Printed in the United States
213047BV00006B/2/P